by the same author

FRINCK: A LIFE IN THE DAY OF and
    SUMMER WITH MONIKA (novel and poems)
WATCHWORDS (poems)
AFTER THE MERRYMAKING (poems)
OUT OF SEQUENCE (poems)
GIG (poems)
SPORTING RELATIONS (poems)

in the glassroom

ROGER McGOUGH

*Dedicated to those who gaze out of windows
when they should be paying attention*

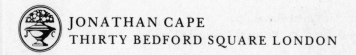

JONATHAN CAPE
THIRTY BEDFORD SQUARE LONDON

First published in 1976
Reprinted 1978
© 1976 by Roger McGough

JONATHAN CAPE LTD, 30 BEDFORD SQUARE LONDON WC1

'Goodbat Nightman' was first published in *Mersey Sound*,
Penguin Modern Poets Book 10, 1967, and
'Three Rusty Nails' under the title
'Mother, there's a strange man' in *The Liverpool Scene*,
Donald Carroll Ltd, 1967

British Library Cataloguing in Publication Data

McGough, Roger
    In the glassroom: children's poems.
    ISBN 0-224-01317-3
    1. Title
821'.9'14 PZ 8.3M/

    Children's poetry, English

Printed in Great Britain by
Lowe & Brydone Printers Limited, Thetford, Norfolk

Contents

I say I say I say
A funny thing happened on my way here today
The buildings had hiccoughs, the roads ran away
Buses grew hair in the silliest places
Traffic lights chuckled and pulled funny faces
3-legged lampposts chased little dogs
The moon took a hiding from stars wearing clogs
Policemen threw helmets at innocent stones
As cheeky boys laughed and broke words with bones
The bells in the batfry have started to roar
A poet's not safe out alone any more.

First Day at School

A millionbillionwillion miles from home
Waiting for the bell to go. (To go where?)
Why are they all so big, other children?
So noisy? So much at home they
must have been born in uniform
Lived all their lives in playgrounds
Spent the years inventing games
that don't let me in. Games
that are rough, that swallow you up.

And the railings.
All around, the railings.
Are they to keep out wolves and monsters?
Things that carry off and eat children?
Things you don't take sweets from?
Perhaps they're to stop us getting out
Running away from the lessins. Lessin.
What does a lessin look like?
Sounds small and slimy.
They keep them in glassrooms.
Whole rooms made out of glass. Imagine.

I wish I could remember my name
Mummy said it would come in useful.
Like wellies. When there's puddles.
Yellowwellies. I wish she was here.
I think my name is sewn on somewhere
Perhaps the teacher will read it for me.
Tea-cher. The one who makes the tea.

Streemin

Im in the botom streme
Which meens Im not brigth
dont like reading
cant hardly write

but all these divishns
arnt reely fair
look at the cemtery
no streemin there

Bestlooking Girl

Im the bestlooking girl in our year
It's a fact

All the lads fancy me, and the girls
Are jealous

Mind you, all the lads here are rubbish
Just like kids

My boyfriend is a deejay in town
In a club

He sounds american but he's not
He's scottish

He wants to get on Radio One
Then TV

He thinks I'm 16 so I let him
Now and then

Nooligan

I'm a nooligan
dont give a toss
in our class
I'm the boss
(well, one of them)

I'm a nooligan
got a nard 'ead
step out of line
and youre dead
(well, bleedin)

I'm a nooligan
I spray me name
all over town
footballs me game
(well, watchin)

I'm a nooligan
violence is fun
gonna be a nassassin
or a nired gun
(well, a soldier)

Out and About, the Lads

pants flapping round legpoles
like denim flags

necks open to the wind
their element

boots the colour of raw liver
boss the pavement

out and about
the lads

voices raised like fists
tattooed with curses

outnumbered rivals
they take in their stride

lampposts and pillarboxes
step aside

out and about
the lads

thick as thieves
and every one a star

Paul uses a knife
you dont feel a thing

Des the best speller
the aerosol king

out and about
the lads

cornered young
they will live their lives in corners

umpteenagers
out on a spree

looking for the likes
of you and me

out and about
the lads.

The Lesson

A poem that raises the question:
Should there be capital punishment in schools?

Chaos ruled OK in the classroom
as bravely the teacher walked in
the havocwreakers ignored him
his voice was lost in the din

'The theme for today is violence
and homework will be set
I'm going to teach you a lesson
one that you'll never forget'

He picked on a boy who was shouting
and throttled him then and there
then garrotted the girl behind him
(the one with grotty hair)

Then sword in hand he hacked his way
between the chattering rows
'First come, first severed' he declared
'fingers, feet, or toes'

He threw the sword at a latecomer
it struck with deadly aim
then pulling out a shotgun
he continued with his game

The first blast cleared the backrow
(where those who skive hang out)
they collapsed like rubber dinghies
when the plugs pulled out

'Please may I leave the room sir?'
a trembling vandal enquired
'Of course you may' said teacher
put the gun to his temple and fired

The Head popped a head round the doorway
to see why a din was being made
nodded understandingly
then tossed in a grenade

And when the ammo was well spent
with blood on every chair
Silence shuffled forward
with its hands up in the air

The teacher surveyed the carnage
the dying and the dead
He waggled a finger severely
'Now let that be a lesson' he said

He who owns the Whistle, rules the World

january wind and the sun
playing truant again.
Rain beginning to scratch
its fingernails across
the blackboard sky

in the playground
kids divebomb, corner
at silverstone or execute
traitors. Armed
with my Acme Thunderer
I step outside,
take a deep breath
and bring the world
to a standstill

Rainymorning

the sky
is pretty mad about something
and i don't blame it.
Thats no weather to be out in.

                                    Out in
the yard that pretends its a garden
the green bits buckle
under the downslaught.

After the rain
come the violins.
Bluebells
shake their tiny heads in disbelief
Birds
come out of hiding
sing the first song of morning
then fly off to the motorway

to watch motorists queueingt^{op_i}leup

Yellow Book:

You stand behind the curtain
your ear to the windowpane
Listening for secrets
in the chatter of the rain

which clouds got married
which ones left his wife
which winds joined the army
which ones lost its life

You love the latest scandals
you never miss a word
And when the raindrops go away
you write down all you've heard

which mountain keeps a mistress
which ones growing old
which flowers pregnant
which ones got a cold

You keep a little yellow book
and when the windows rattle
You eavesdrop and you then record
nature's tittle-tattle.

which trees bought a new dress
which ones looking pale
which rivers ran away to sea
which ones gone to jail

One night I took your yellow book
and tried to read in vain
For who but you can understand
the language of the rain?

Spaced-out Summer Poem

slow paces

cloud

patches of sky

cat chases

swallows

catches a fly

        slow paces

        patches

        of cloud in the sky

        cat chases

        catches

        swallows a fly

Autumn Poem

litter

    is

        turning

          brown

            and

              the

                road

                  above

                is

              filled

            with

         hitch

       hikers

     heading

south

,

twould be nice to be
an apostrophe
floating
above an s
hovering
like a paper kite
in between the its
eavesdropping, tiptoeing
high above the thats
an inky comet
spiralling
the highest tossed
of hats

♩

I wish I were a crotchet
I'd sing and dance and play
among the dotted minims
all the livelong day

I'd swing from stave to stave
up and down I'd climb
Then crawl from bar to bar
singing all the time

I wish I were a crotchet
or a semi-breve
I'd find a lady quaver
and her I'd never leave

We'd run around the manuscript
a pair of little ravers
get married pianissimo
and raise lots of semi-quavers

Words . . . Poems

Look after
the
and the
        will
take care
of themselves

A Good Poem

I like a good poem
one with lots of fighting
in it. Blood, and the
clanging of armour.   Poems

against Scotland are good,
and poems that defeat
the French with crossbows.
I don't like poems that

aren't about anything.
Sonnets are wet and
a waste of time.
Also poems that don't

know how to rhyme.
If I was a poem
I'd play football and
get picked for England.

Footy Poem

I'm an ordinary feller 6 days of the week
But Saturday turn into a football freak.
I'm a schizofanatic, sad but it's true
One half of me's red, and the other half's blue.

I can't make me mind up which team to support
Whether to lean to starboard or port
I'd be bisexual if I had time for sex
Cos it's Goodison one week and Anfield the next.

But the worst time of all is Derby day
One half of me's at home and the other's away
So I get down there early all ready for battle
With me rainbow scarf and me two-tone rattle.

And I'm shouting for Latchford and I'm shouting for
    Hughes
'Come on de Pool' — 'Gerrin dere Blues'
'Give it ter Keegan' — 'Worra puddin'
'King of der Kop' — All of a sudden — Wop!
'Goal!' — 'Offside!'

And after the match as I walk back alone
It's argue, argue all the way home
Some nights when I'm drunk I've even let fly
An give meself a poke in the eye

But in front of the fire watchin' 'Match of the Day'
Tired but happy, I look at it this way:
Part of me's lost and part of me's won
I've had twice the heartaches — but I've had twice the fun.

Estate

Mother!
They're building a towncentre in the bedroom
A carpark in the lounge, it's a sin.

There's a block of flats going up in the toilet
What a shocking estate we are in.

Cupboard Love

Recoin some phrases
to sing your praises
but you don't want to know

touch your arm
say what's the harm
but you just want to go

you're unbending
no happyending
you make your way to the door

(things could be worse
I've pinched your purse
it's with all the rest in the drawer)

Chicken

Some nights
when I've had a few
I ask the world
to take off its coat
and step outside.
Luckily for you
it's always chickened out.

Goodbat Nightman

God bless all policemen
and fighters of crime,
May thieves go to jail
for a very long time.

They've had a hard day
helping clean up the town,
Now they hang from the mantelpiece
both upside down.

A glass of warm blood
and then straight up the stairs,
Batman and Robin
are saying their prayers.

*   *   *

They've locked all the doors
and they've put out the bat,
Put on their batjamas
(They like doing that)

They've filled their batwater-bottles
made their batbeds,
With two springy battresses
for sleepy batheads.

They're closing red eyes
and they're counting black sheep,
Batman and Robin
are falling asleep.

Catching up on Sleep

i go to bed early
to catch up on my sleep
            but my sleep
is a slippery customer
it bobs and weaves
            and leaves
me exhausted. It
side steps my clumsy tackles
with ease.   Bed
raggled I drag
myself to my knees.

The sheep are countless
I pretend to snore
yearn for chloroform
or a sock on the jaw
body sweats heart beats
there is Panic in the Sheets
until
as dawn slopes up the stairs
to set me free
unawares
sleep catches up on me

Wink

I took 40 winks
yesterday afternoon
and another 40 today.
In fact I get through
about 280 winks a week.
Which is about 14,560
winks a year.
(The way I'm going on
I'll end up looking like a wink)

Kyrie

There was a porter
who had ideas
high above his railway station
always causing righteous indignation

he wanted to be
giant amongst men
saviour come again to earth
but his teachings only met with mirth

one bright winters morn
packed in his job
believed the world needed him
dedicated his life to fighting sin

the second day out
crossing the road
apparently in Stockport town
a diesel lorry swerved and knocked him down

back at the station
all the porters
wore mourning masks on their faces
and all agreed he should have stuck to cases

Three Rusty Nails

Mother, there's a strange man
Waiting at the door
With a familiar sort of face
You feel you've seen before.

Says his name is Jesus
Can we spare a couple of bob
Says he's been made redundant
And now can't find a job.

Yes I think he is a foreigner
Egyptian or a Jew
Oh aye, and that reminds me
He'd like some water too.

Well shall I give him what he wants
Or send him on his way?
O.K. I'll give him 5p
Say that's all we've got today.

And I'll forget about the water
I suppose it's a bit unfair
But honest, he's filthy dirty
All beard and straggly hair.

*   *   *

Mother, he asked about the water
I said the tank had burst
Anyway I gave him the coppers
That seemed to quench his thirst.

He said it was little things like that
That kept him on the rails
Then he gave me his autographed picture
And these three rusty nails.

Newsflash

In a dawn raid
early this morning
Gendarmes arrested
a family of four
found bathing
on a secluded beach
outside Swansea

Later in the day
tracker dogs
led German police officers
to the scene of a picnic
near Brighton.
Salmonpaste sandwiches
and a thermos of tea
were discovered.
The picnickers however
escaped.

The Commission

In this poem there is a table
Groaning with food.
There is also a child
Groaning for lack of food.
The food is beautifully photographed
The meat more succulent
The fruit as juicy
As you are likely to see.
(The child is sketched in lightly
She is not important.)
The photograph is to be used
In a glossy magazine
As part of a campaign
Advertising after-dinner mints.

This evening the photographer
In receipt of his fee
Celebrates by dining with friends
In a famous West End restaurant.
Doodling on the napkin between courses
The photographer, always creative,
Draws a little Asian girl,
Naked, wide-eyed, pleading.
The photographer is pleased.
He has an idea for the next commission,
The one for famine relief.
The tandoori arrives
He puts away his pen
And picks up a fork.

A Brown Paper Carrierbag

IN THE TIME . . .

    a spider's web woven across
    the plateglass window shivers snaps
    and sends a shimmering haze of lethal stars
    across the crowded restaurant

IN THE TIME IT TAKES . . .

    jigsaw pieces of shrapnel
    glide gently towards children
    tucking in   to the warm flesh
    a terrible hunger sated

IN THE TIME IT TAKES TO PUT DOWN . . .

    on the pavement
    people come apart   slowly
    at first
    only the dead not screaming

IN THE TIME IT TAKES TO PUT DOWN
A BROWN PAPER CARRIERBAG.

Science, where are you?

I started smoking young. The Big C
didn't scare me. By the time
I was old enough to get it,
Science would have found the cure.
'Ad astra per angina' was the
family motto, and thrombosis
an heirloom I didn't care to inherit.
But I didn't worry. By the time
I was old enough to face it
St Science would surely have
slain that particular dragon.

Suddenly I'm old enough . . .
Science, where are you Science?
What have you been doing
all these years? Were you playing
out when you should have been
doing your homework? Daydreaming
in class when you should
have been paying attention?
Have you been wasting your time
and worse still, wasting mine?

When you left school did you
write scripts for 'Tomorrow's World'
before being seduced by a starlet
from a soap ad? Lured by the
bright lights of commercialism
did you invent screwtop bottles,
self-adhesive wallpaper, nonstick
pans, chocolate that melts
in the mouth not the hands?

Kingsize fags, tea-leaves in bags
cars and bras sycophantic
Oxo cubes now transatlantic?

(Or worse still
did you fall
for a sweet talkin'
warmonger? Have a
consciencectomy
and practise
death control?)

The Arts I expected nothing from.
Good company when they're sober
but totally unreliable. But
Science, I expected more from you.
A bit dull perhaps, but steady.
Plodding, but getting there in the end.
Now the end limps into view
and where are you? Cultivating
cosmic pastures new? Biting off
more Space than you can chew?
Science you're needed here, come down
and stay. I've got this funny pain
and it won't go awa

                    a
                      a
                        a
                          g
                            g
                              g
                                h
                                  h
                                    h

39

Mad Ad

A Madison Avenue whizzkid
thought it a disgrace
That no one had exploited
the possibilities in space
Discussed it with a client
who agreed and very soon
A thousand miles of neontubing
were transported to the moon.

Now no one can ignore it
the product's selling fine
The night they turned the moon
into a Coca-Cola sign.

Near to You

America's the land of milk and honey
Australia's healthy and continually sunny
The living in Sweden is clean and sleek
The food in France is gastronomique

Japan's got geishas and the fastest train
China's got noodles and chicken chow mein
When the monsoon's there India's fine
Israel's got Moshe Dayan

Africa looks to a future exciting
Spain's got sherry, flies and bullfighting
Eskimos are tough and used to roughing
Turkey is full of chestnut stuffing

The Belgians invented the Brussels sprout
Germans lieben lederhosen und sauerkraut
Greece abounds in classical ruins
Russia's violinists play the loveliest tuins

In Bermuda it's sunny beaches and foam
In Switzerland it's gnome sweet gnome
Italian girls make a di fantastic lovers
Danes are mustard under the covers

From old Hawaii to New Nepal
Foreigners seem to have it all
So if everything abroad is as good as they say
Why do we Britons in Britain stay?

The answer is (and I'm sure it's true)
That all of us want to be near to you

Postcard Poems

No. 1
iceflow sighted
off Newquay
and they're surfing
in the High Street.
It's women and children first
in the T.V. lounge
and at lunchtime
there was an oilslick
in my soup
'Having a wonderful time
Wish you were her'

No. 2
its olé
to bed
and olé
to rise
only the tourists
outnumber the flies

Conversation on a Train

I'm Shirley, she's Mary.
We're from Swansea
(if there was a horse there
it'd be a one-horse town
but there isn't even that).
We're going to Blackpool
Just the week. A bit late I know
But then there's the Illuminations
Isn't there? No, never been before.
Paris last year. Didn't like it.
Too expensive and nothing there really.

Dirty old train isn't it?
And not even a running buffet.
Packet of crisps would do
Change at Crewe
Probably have to wait hours
For the connection, and these cases
Are bloody heavy.
And those porters only want tipping.
Reminds you of Paris that does
Tip tip tip all the time.
Think you're made of money over there.

Toy factory, and Mary works in a shop.
Grocers. Oh it's not bad
Mind you the money's terrible.
Where are you from now?
Oh aye, diya know the Beatles then?
Liar!
And what do you do for a living?
You don't say.
Diya hear that Mary?
Well I hope you don't go home
And write a bloody poem about us.

Smithereens

I spend my days
collecting smithereens.
I find them on buses
in department stores
and on busy pavements

At restaurant tables
I pick up the leftovers
of polite conversation
At railway stations
the tearful debris
of parting lovers.

I pocket my eavesdroppings
and store them away.
I make things out of them.
Nice things, sometimes.
Sometimes odd, like this.

KURT
B.P.
MUNGO
AND
ME

1

In Search of Adventure

It must have been dead miserable up in the sky because the rain couldn't get to the ground quick enough. It was puking it down. Although it was a Friday afternoon, the streets were deserted. Boutiques, shoeshops, record shops, delicatessens were crammed with moist tramps, traffic wardens, hotdogmen and newspaper sellers, all pretending to buy things. Even shoplifters, coats stuffed with loot, postponed their dash for freedom and hovered, at risk, near the exits.

But it took more than a torrential downpour to dampen the spirits of Three Lads in search of adventure. B.P., Kurt and Mungo battled bravely up Castle Street.

'What a lousy day to start a story,' moaned Kurt. His mates nodded, wetly.

'What do you think we should do?'

'Tell him,' said B.P.

'Deffo,' agreed Mungo. Kurt stopped and turned towards me.

'Look, can't we wait till the rain goes off?'

It seemed a reasonable request. That was certainly no weather to be out in, fiction or no fiction.

'O.K.,' I said 'Go and dry out and I'll bring you back later.'

They disappeared, leaving only the rain soaking into the page.

2

Flags

The sun was cracking the flags. There could be little doubt about that. The Three Lasd were sitting on the steps outside St Luke's Church. It was only half-past ten in the morning but already the sun was cracking the flags.

'Why are there so many flags about?' asked Mungo.

'Dunno, must be a flag day or something,' said B.P. They relaxed into silence for a few minutes before Kurt spoke; I didn't catch what he said because my attention was drawn to a round of drunks on a bench about twenty-five yards away. One was an old man, the kind that gives tramps a bad name, but the others were youngish, in the dying roar of their twenties I'd guess, though it was difficult to tell because their faces were hard set and lined as if they had spent their lives walking into a harsh wind.

They were drinking cheap sherry and cider. They weren't celebrating anything or having a good time, but nor were they miserable either. Drink can take leave of your senses. They were just sitting and drinking, and listening to the sun cracking the flags.

3

When you don't have any money, not a penny, then a day can take a long time to get on its bike and ride away. A town can be an unfriendly place when so much of it is closed to you. You can look but don't touch, smell the chips but not buy them, see the cinema posters but not the film, run riot with the soccer fans but not get to the match.

Of course you can steal things and bunk into places. Lots of people do, quite nice friendly people some of them. But Kurt, Mungo and B.P. aren't like that. I've made them honest. I've given them hope for the Future. They remain optimistic even when the going is rough. When they leave school they'll have trouble finding jobs, but at least they have a Future. Any Future is better than no Future. Like breath, even bad breath is better than no breath at all.

4

The Future

The Future does not look like this . . .

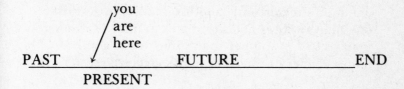

The Future looks more like this . . .

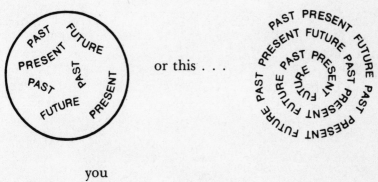

or this . . .

or this . . . here

You could say that if this book is TIME, the pages that you have read so far are the PAST. The page that you are looking at now is the PRESENT, and the rest of the book is the FUTURE.

But that can't be true because I know what is on the other pages, therefore it can't be the Future, it's all the same.

One man's Past is another man's Future
one man's pork is another man's poison
one man's dogfood is another man's dinner
one man's drink is another man's bathwater
one man's terrorism is another man's patriotism
one man's wife is another man's mother is another
man's sister is another man's mistress is another
man's etcetera is another man's etcetera etcetera

*　　*　　*　　*　　*

5

The Three Alds were on the top deck of a number 73
bus going into town. They were reading a book that
someone had left behind (whether or not on purpose
we will never know). It was this book.

I could pretend that they were enjoying it.
Chuckling heartily over its many nuances and shifts of
direction; laughing aloud at the cascading puns and
razor-sharp wit. I could pretend but I won't. They
weren't enjoying it. They found it irritating in the
extreme.

In fact Kurt turned stroppy:

'Look, this is all very well, but why couldn't we be
characters in a proper story? You know, three
intelligent public schoolboys from nice homes with
sisters whose hobbies are ballet and horseriding.'

To be honest, this took me by surprise because I
didn't think they would be into that schoolboy
adventure stuff — bullies, dorms and tuckshops. Prep,
pigtails and hockeysticks. They'd obviously read some
of those old Billy-Bunter-type annuals and been
impressed by that cosy world where the goody goodies
win out and the cowards get their comeuppance.*

Mungo backed up his mate.

'Kurt's right. Why can't we be called Jonathan,
Nicholas and Simon and have thrilling adventures and
win through against rotters and live happy ever after?'

'All we're doin'', said B.P. 'is piddlin' about.' I had
to admit they weren't the moulds out of which heroes
are usually cast.

B.P.** was black, had an Afro haircut, and was so tall and thin that if he lay at the foot of a Belisha beacon he looked like its shadow.

Mungo was average.

Kurt (who wasn't average) looked a bit like you.***

In fact, the three of them were so ordinary and dull that I began to wonder why I had invented them. Anyway I had, and I was getting used to them. Given time, I reckoned I might even grow to like them.

Of course I didn't say any of this to them because I didn't want to hurt their feelings. So I told them how witty and lovable they were and how important they would be in the excitement-packed story that was about to unfold.****

Why else, I reasoned, would they be on the top deck of a number 73 bus going into town?

They seemed reasonably satisfied, and sliding the book back into a crack between the seats settled down to a game of asterisks.*****

---

*   Taken from the Famous quotation by Mae West:
          'Comeuppance see me sometime.'
**   B.P. Abbrev. for Butcher's Pencil. Nickname derived
          from the expression 'I've seen more meat on a Butcher's
          Pencil.'
***   Unless of course you are a girl, in which case he looks like
          any boy of your choice.
****   See Chapter Eight.
*****   Asterisks. Little things that look like this ****.

6

Jonesy is a nooligan
Jonesy is a savidge
Jonesy's 'ead is mader wood
and stuffed wi' pickled cabbidge

Jonesy is a nooligan. He is still only fifteen, at the time
of writing, but already he has a criminal record AS
LONG AS . . .   (a) my arm
              (b) your arm
              (c) you don't tell anybody.

He is standing on the corner of Lark Lane and
Albert Street waiting for a handbag, stuffed with
pound notes, to jump into his hands via a defenceless
old lady. He chooses his victims with care. He prefers
them to look like the old gasbag from number 17,
whom he can't stand because she used to babysit on
him.
   Jonesy has learned patience. Patience is a virtue. If
Jonesy has a virtue he can't be all bad. No one is all
bad.
   Along the road comes Mrs Lloyd. She is thinking
about her granddaughter and what to buy her for her
birthday.*

Jonesy is a nooligan
Jonesy is a creep
Jonesy burgles houses
While everyone's asleep

He moves quicker than greased thunder, snatches the bag, and is up the street and away into the distance like dots . . . . . .

Mrs. Lloyd is shocked. Is upset. She begins to tremble. Shake. She staggers about the pavement not knowing whether to cry out for help or burst into tears. She is embarrassed. Passers by pass by.

*   Her birthday is on November 18th, by the way, if you want to send a card.

To the Rescue

The Three Slad had just got off the number 73 bus
when they witnessed the Great Handbag Robbery.

(At last, the comic book chance they'd been waiting
for.)

'Crumbs, it's that rotter Jonesy up to his beastly tricks
again' shouted Mungo, in his best Port Out Starboard
Home voice.

The villain was 20 yards clear up the road.

'Come on chaps, let's nail him once and for all.'

The Magnificent Three fullpelted after him. B.P.,
the fleetest of feet, was first upon him. He grabbed a
handful of greasy hair.

'Right, you bounder, hold still there.'

Mungo wellied him in the groin.

'It's cads like you that get the School a bad name.'

Kurt wrestled the handbag free while Jonesy cursed
and struggled with the blue-haired curly-eyed heroes of
Denim Street Comprehensive.

Finally, with the swift, graceful movements of the
superbly trained vandal, Jonesy broke loose, legged
down an entry and out of the chapter.

'Shall we go after him?' asked Mungo.

'Nah, let him go,' said Kurt. 'Lets go and give this
back to the old lady. That is, if we can find her.'

Although there seemed to be a lot of people
suddenly milling about, there was no old lady.

'Have a look at her pension book, that'll have her
address,' suggested B.P.

Our three brave champions of justice were busily
rummaging through Mrs Lloyd's handbag when the
Panda car drew up.

8

See Chapter Three

A girl called Sharon is sitting in a Wimpy Bar
waiting for the love of her young life. Already he is
an hour late. He has good reason to be.

Sharon has gone over in her head, a hundred times,
what she will say to Jonesy. How she will tell him. She
orders another coffee and a piece of home-made apple
pie. Factory freshish. Nearly ten to eight. She will give
him until eight o'clock and then go home.

> 'I'm having a baby'
> '*We're* having a baby'
> 'Guess what, I'm pregnant'
> (Oh god, what will gran say?)

A police car elbows its way through the traffic
outside, followed by two ambulances and a fire engine.
The coffee tastes bitter, the pie sickly.

> 'Of course I'm sure'
> 'We'll get married, but only if you want to'
> 'No I want to keep it . . . I don't care,
> I'm going to keep it.'
> 'You do love me don't you?'
> (Oh god, what will Jonesy say?)

She wonders if people can tell. Tell by her complexion.
Her fidgeting. 'Pregnant.' She mouths the word to
herself, repeats is like a prayer. 'Preg . . . nant . . .
egnant . . . eg . . . egg.'

'Egg.' 'Embryo.' Her body has taken in a lodger.
Someone has come to stay for a while. Quietly, without
breathing, she tries to feel its presence. Outside
another fire engine hurries past, trying to catch up
with its mate.

'We can live at ours till you get a job'
'There's only me and me gran'
'You'll like her when you meet her'
(Oh god, what will they say at school?)

Sharon lives with her gran. Sharon's gran is Mrs
Lloyd. At twenty past eight Sharon pays her bill and
leaves.

10

All's well that ends

Owing to the gravity of the charge (Mrs Lloyd had staggered into the road, and an oil tanker swerving to avoid her had skidded into a chemical plant which, on exploding, had wiped out half of Liverpool), the case had attracted much publicity.

The Magistrate was pronouncing sentence before a packed court. It was so quiet you could hear a gum drop.

'. . . too much of this sort of think going on . . . streets not safe to walk on . . . if I ruled the world . . . make an example of you . . . 30 years' imprisonment.'

A gasp went around the courtroom.

'Get that gasp out of here,' ordered the Magistrate.

Two policemen went quickly into action and removed the gasp, still struggling, from the courtroom.

'But we're innocent,' cried Mungo.

'We were only trying to help,' said Kurt, close to tears.

'That's what they all say,' snapped the Magistrate. 'Take them away.'

'Ahray . . . Ahray, that's not fair,' B.P. looked at me accusingly.

'We didn't ask to be in this lousy story. We've had no fun at all. No money, nothing to eat, didn't get off with any girls, and now you're sending us to prison for 30 years.'

Kurt chipped in:

'And you know damn well it was Jonesy what did it in Chapter 5.'

'It was Chapter 6 actually,' I corrected.

'Silence in Court,' shouted the ruddy-voiced Magistrate. He was beginning to get on my nerves.

'Who do you think you're talking to?' I said.

'You,' said the Magistrate.

'Are you indeed, well I'll soon show you who's author around here.' And with that turned him into a bluebottle which buzzed around the courtroom for a few minutes before disappearing for ever through an open window.

I turned my attention back to the boys. I suppose I had been hard on them, a little thoughtless perhaps. I decided to throw the ball back into their Magistrates Court.

Did they have any ideas on how to end the story? The suggestions came thick and fast.

(i) Jonesy owns up

(ii) Mrs Lloyd arrives at the last minute to give evidence clearing the accused

(iii) The heroes are commended by the police and rewarded for recovering the handbag

(iv) They receive £1,000 each as compensation for wrongful arrest

(v) Mrs Lloyd forgives Jonesy who then marries Sharon. B.P. is best man

(vi) Jonesy gets run over by an ambulance. Sharon marries Mungo

(vii) Sharon dies having the baby. Heartbroken, Jonesy commits suicide/becomes a priest/joins the army

(viii) Kurt becomes . . .

They were enjoying themselves at last. It was getting late. I left them to it.